LUCK IS THE HOOK

Imtiaz Dharker

LUCK IS THE HOOK

BLOODAXE BOOKS

ISBN: 978 1 78037 218 1

First published 2018 by
Bloodaxe Books Ltd,
Eastburn,
South Park,
Hexham,
Northumberland NE46 1BS.

www.bloodaxebooks.com
For further information about Bloodaxe titles
please visit our website or write to
the above address for a catalogue.

Supported using public funding by
**ARTS COUNCIL
ENGLAND**

Cover design: Neil Astley & Pamela Robertson-Pearce.

Printed in Great Britain by Bell & Bain Limited, Glasgow, Scotland, on
acid-free paper sourced from mills with FSC chain of custody certification.

for Ava, Luca, Sofia

CONTENTS

10 Chaudhri Sher Mobarik looks at the loch

11 The Knot

12 Stitch

15 Snag

16 Fankle

17 Always, snow

19 Kissing strangers

21 Thaw

22 To have all this

23 Vespare

27 Seal, River Clyde

28 Letters to Glasgow

31 Bairn

32 Long

33 Arc

35 Made, Unmade

37 A Haunting

41 Six pomegranate seeds

42 Underground

45 The Letter

46 Sixty seconds

47 Sticks

48 Beak

49 Fix

51 Six rings

52 Rings

53 A haunting of words

55 Flight

56 Hell-raiser

57 Haunted

59 Warning

60 The trick

61 Lapis Lazuli
62 The Elephant is walking on the River Thames
63 Hide
65 First sight, through falling snow
66 Fair
67 Night vision
69 Mr Wisdom Looks for China by the Thames
71 Larks
73 Heavenly Emporium
74 If you are looking for Wisdom
75 m) Those that have just broken the vase
77 Cherub, St Paul's
79 Checkout
81 Flight Radar
82 Unexploded
84 Exploded
85 Channel of vision
88 Brutal
89 The Elephants are on the Piccadilly Line
91 The Fabrick
92 Ringing the changes
93 The sound of your name
95 Bloom
96 Close to the sun
97 Wolf, Words
99 What will you tell the children?
101 Out of line
102 Gurh and ghee
103 The Jump
105 Send this
106 This line, that thread
107 The garden gnomes are on their mobile phones
109 Drain
110 Double
111 3 a.m., the radio on

113   Estuary

115   This Tide of Humber

125   *Acknowledgements*

These ambiguities, redundancies, and deficiencies recall those attributed by Dr Franz Kuhn to a certain Chinese encyclopaedia called the Heavenly Emporium of Benevolent Knowledge. In its distant pages it is written that animals are divided into (a) those that belong to the emperor; (b) embalmed ones; (c) those that are trained; (d) suckling pigs; (e) mermaids; (f) fabulous ones; (g) stray dogs; (h) those that are included in this classification; (i) those that tremble as if they were mad; (j) innumerable ones; (k) those drawn with a very fine camel's-hair brush; (l) etcetera; (m) those that have just broken the flower vase; (n) those that at a distance resemble flies.

JORGE LUIS BORGES
from *Otras Inquisiciones*
'El idioma analitico de John Wilkins' (1942)
translated by Eliot Weinberger

Chaudhri Sher Mobarik looks at the loch

Light shakes out the dishrag sky
and scatters the water with sequins. *Look, hen!*
says my father, *Loch Lomond!* as if
it were all his doing, as if he owned it,
laird of Lomond, laird of the language.
He is proud to say *hen* and even more *loch*
with an *och* not an *ock*, to speak
proper Glaswegian like a true-born Scot,
and he makes the right sound at the back
of the throat because he can say *khush*
and *khwab* and *khamosh*, because the sounds
for happy and dream are the words that swim
in the water for him, so he says it again,
Hen! Look! The loch!

The Knot

At Loch Lomond they were king and queen to me,
laying out their bounty on the brae
after the queasy ride from Glasgow, we
children making sick-stops on the way.

Tumbled out, we sprawled at the water's mouth
where light ate shade and made us ravenous.
With a flourish, Her Majesty untied the cloth
to set parathas free. She did, she does,

undoes this deep red knot of hurt in the heart.
Today, when scars have been allowed to deepen
around a silence, wrenching our lives apart,
she has come back to us at the loch to open

out the tangle of her dying, the mistake,
the high, the low, the road we did not take.

Stitch

Cathy's mother says
she is her sweet heart.
My mother says I am a piece of her liver.

Cathy has an ice blue cardigan.
My mother holds Cathy still
in front of her, and studies the stitches

with her eyes screwed up. She
measures me with the span of her hand
and marches me over the bridge

to Argyle Street for wool and needles.
Sitting by the fireplace, she is fierce,
unwinds the skein to a ball

off my arms, slips one, purls one,
unravels, starts again,
needles clicking, clacking

in time to the pattern in her head,
the shape of the life she is plotting
for me, knitting herself into me.

Done, she holds the cardigan
over my chest, a perfect copy
of Cathy's, but red.

The edges wriggle more
because hers is machine-made
and mine is worked by hand.

Years later, when I leave, my mother cries
on the phone, and says her liver
has been torn apart.

Snag

Afterwards they said
there were snags in the liver
that spelt out a name.

Fankle

One end was *I want*
           and the other was *we don't*,
one thread was *please*
           and the other was *not today*,
one strand was *I think*
           and the other was *don't be daft*,
one cast on with *but*
           and cast off with *obey*.
In the middle of it all
           was the knot, the coiled snare
of *if you love me*,
           if you really care,
that started off free
           till there was hell to pay
and the answer to *why*
           was always *log kya kahenge*,
the beginning and the end,
           what will people say.
What will people say
           when they see
my running line,
           your cunning hook,
my lost sign,
           your last look
fankled up so tight
           that even if I have escaped,
your arms twine
           around my neck
and pull me back?

Always, snow

It goes on
falling on wet pavements,

silent as the words you do not say,
weightless as the thought

that never reaches skin,
cold as the space you leave behind,

lost just as it touches down,
gone before it has a chance

to kiss the ground.

Kissing strangers

Sometimes the mouth is so unknown
that kissing it is a flight
to another country,

the unexpected dip above the lip,
the wicked skid round corners,
the corners tilted up

to tip you straight into the place
where the accent changes.
Why talk to strangers when

there's kissing to be done instead?
Your mother's lipstick blazes
Rimini Red on your lips

and some of it on the cheek of the boy
outside the Italian café
where the music plays

T'ho veduta.
T'ho sequita.
T'ho fermata.

T'ho baciata.
Eri piccola, piccola, piccola,
così!

Your mouth is still cold
from the ice-cream cone, his warm
with raspberry blood

and that other thing you can't get
your tongue around, that comes
from somewhere blue,

Azzurro,
il pomeriggio è troppo azzurro
e lungo per me.

Mi accorgo
di non avere più risorse,
senza di te,

where you have gone in your head,
where the language plays by different rules
and your only signposts are the stars.

Thaw

The day blows a fuse. You walk out,
your breath a snow-storm surging
round your mouth, your tracks a baffled
argument in black and white.

Outside has switched to night
too soon. The window loses
sight of you and turns into a mirror
in mid-afternoon. You come back in.

Frost filaments in your hair, eyebrows
picked out in crystal, every fibre
on your coat is live, sleeves and shoulders
pricked with ice and points of light.

You are electric.
You bring the outside in
and the whole room is shocked
into winter.

You smell of cold. My face
close up to yours, I am singed,
locked in to you.
This early nightfall, this

dark-too-soon, untimely as it is,
takes us straight to bed, throws back
the sheet and draws us in to thaw
your frozen feet between my feet.

To have all this

The certainty of waking in your eyes,
you in mine; the quiet drifting
in and out of each other's sleep, this calm;

these mornings – count them –
when snowfall hushes the outside
and the bed is our only country;

these moments when you stir
and I know how your arm will lift into
the glow, the exact turn of your wrist,

this hand that draws me daily in,
takes me apart and makes me up
again, a little changed;

this distance, the flurry of messages
you send to my phone, a scroll
of the times you think my name.

this coming back: you
at the ticket barrier, your face
tilted up to find me;

this standing at the edge,
guessing at the clouds that move
through you, the earth breathing.

To have all this:
to hold you,
to be held.

Vespare

A blur of white, a wipe on a screen
that could lead to almost anything.

The next scene could be an empty street
that stays empty, or he could ride in.

He might stop at the traffic-lights,
wait for green, and speed on.

But what if, instead, before
the lights change, she steps out?

Out on the road,
into the frame,

one of those shots
where only slow-motion will do

justice to the tilt of her head,
the reflection of her in his visor?

Chance plays a part in all these things.
Who can say where it will start,

what sound will be the trigger, what scent,
which arrow in the heart?

What if the white van had pulled
in front instead of to his right?

He catches sight of the profile. She
turns to look, already struck

by the Italian accent
of his engine, and with any luck

he might be Gregory Peck
in Roman Holiday.

His head spinning,
he takes off his helmet.

She smiles
at the scooter. She likes its style.

The white van man says,
Mate, I think you've pulled,

so he pulls over,
well pleased with himself,

and that is where they meet,
under the traffic-lights

that change their luck
from red to amber to green.

The rest is a wipe on a screen
as the two go speeding

round a corner
to reach this place, together.

They turn to us in a blur of white
and we feel the whole world turning

under the wheels,
the dizzy curve of the horizon,

and the sound track
is church bells ringing.

It may not be all
easy riding.

There may be moments
that seem to skid, or stall,

or need a kick-start,
others zooming and weaving,

but there will always be days
like these, well-timed,

well-tuned and sweet
as that first kiss,

when life buzzes along,
and sings like a Vespa.

Seal, River Clyde

Flourishing, aye, its glass filled with dazzle
all the way up to the sky, *Glas-cu* greened
as if St Mungo has just passed by. It might
have been just yesterday he broke a branch
off a tree and it burst into flame
and could this be the tree, could this be the tree?

Out of the tree a robin sang
its last song into the exhausted air,
but St Mungo was there to pick it up
off the road in case the buses killed it again,
breathing into its mouth, saving its name
and could this be the bird, could this be the bird?

Under Jamaica Bridge, a log rolls and turns
into a shining seal. It has swum past the armadillo,
past Glasgow's glass eyes, snakes of children
in high-vis, to search for the live thing
in the water, the salmon that swallowed a ring
and could this be the fish, could this be the fish?

The seal looks at the children and they look back
as if they have a question to ask before the tree
comes alight on the banks of the Clyde, where
the salmon swims to the mouth of the seal
who has something to tell before the bell tolls
and could this be the bell, could this be the bell?

Letters to Glasgow

Heading north is a leap of the heart.
On the map on the phone, the blue dot
is a pulse that crosses the border.

Clouds swing open over the hills
and train chases river, races
after it like a riever,

like a long-distance runner,
breathing hard into the wind
with its flag of light flying behind.

Between home and elsewhere,
between in here and out there,
one journey is layered over the other,

one time on another. Meeting a stranger
on a train, getting to know them better,
is like opening an unexpected letter.

That's me in the garden, and that... I can't tell
if it's Graham or Brian... that's the two of us sat there.
My daughter said, Look at you posing.

In here is a steady hush and a shoosh
that carries her back to the songs she sang
when she was young. She floats

and rocks and someone talks out of the past.
The hum of the train becomes the voice
of her mother, then deepens to be

the voice of her lover so she dreams him back
in the jacket she liked, to share half a sandwich,
tea with milk and one sugar,

his arm brushing hers, and then he will tell her
he went to Ecclefechan before he met her.
The presence of him is the whoosh of wheels

and she is glad he came back for a while.
For a while, in her sleep, she smiles.
The train is a memory-keeper, it carries

something alive, like the words in a letter,
not gathering dust but held in trust.
This is how love moves on and survives.

In the window, her life looks back
at the man on the phone, and reflects his own.
The future comes in and puts down its bags.

Down the carriage, a clicking and pecking
at keyboards, half-heard, half-knowing,
tossed away in the coming and going

like all the other used-up things,
the cardboard wrap, the cellophane,
paper napkins, time-pass, stifled

yawn. The rubbish collector gathers it in,
stopping for breath in the vestibule,
his back to the door, feeling the change

in the sound, the different drumming,
the slip and shiver of in-between
and far below, the long embrace

of wheel and rail. The blue dot is still speeding,
over the screen, sheep are fast
and houses are quicker, going over the edge

with all the lost things at the butt-end of town
where the young fizzle out against walls
sprayed with words in black and red

and the wires are dancing
with the whole of the sky,
meeting and parting, saying goodbye.

We are now approaching, we are now approaching

over the Clyde where the great ships were born,
over the water, a ghostly foghorn,
over the bridge to the city they come,

some of them visiting, some returning.
They take up their baggage and their belongings,
they take up their longings

and the train brings them in to Glasgow Central,
the tall windows, the glass bridge,
the Heilanman's Umbrella lit

to gather them in,
as if someone has waited for them too long,
as if they are love letters, delivered home.

Bairn

There is no way to explain
the light that rises into a room
from the early morning bloom of snow;
through closed lids, the slow dawning
of white. The body is quick to know
the pace of the day has changed, the space
wiped clean to make way for first bird, first song.

There is no way to explain
how, even when the world is wrong,
too spent, too old, it can still be new, renewed
by you, by your first sound, clear note
against the dark. Today, your voice
rising into the house,
the face of the day is changed.

There are things that cleanse the heart.

Long

Streets become lochs in lamplight.
Under the bare trees,
reflections, long as their kiss.

Arc

As I fell, everything fell
out of my mind, the spark
left my eyes, light drained away

and I became a shell, beautiful,
like something that could be filled
with tall tales, new stories, anything

worth imagining. Words
are the pearl. Dive for them
and we become real.

Do you hear my lustre down the line?
Even with all its colour washed away,
wet cloth slapped on stone,

thread beaten too thin,
my voice is still there, an arc
of drops hung in the air, sparkling.

Made, Unmade

Light falls from the sky
like a fresh sheet on a bed
you will not sleep in.

A Haunting

That was where I saw you first,
on the last step of the well,
wet from bathing. Drops of water fell
in an arc from your hair, down
your back, trickling into the cloth
tied tight at your hips. My lips went dry.

My thirst began there and never stopped.
Did you feel how I watched and willed
you to turn? How I waited by the steps
day after day for you to pass,
for the light on your body, the sight of you
sliding into the water, into my heart?

My heart hidden, I learned the art
of making you up in my image,
making something of nothing,
like someone drunk and staggering
from looking at a wineglass,
the wine forbidden.

But I could swear you lifted your head
for the scent of blossoms in my hair.
Kneeling at the brink, I felt you near
and wondered if you would dare
speak. You left. Your eyes
were elsewhere.

You must have heard when I went, the hiss
of scandal. You must have asked
if I was pushed or missed a step
or went willingly over the edge.
You must have wondered
what I felt when I fell. I sank

and sank in the bottomless well
like falling into a night with no stars,
down the shaft of black, the finger
that points out the route to hell.
Not alone, not the first. We are
too many to count, too drowned to tell,

all the lost girls. Gone from the fields
of sugar-cane that stroked our waists
and spoke sweet words, from the houses
that held us too tight and whispered
behind our backs, to this open mouth
with its dangerous breath.

You never come back to the step
where I lie in wait, but other boys do,
wrapping wet cloth around their waists,
laughing with their heads thrown back,
teeth white in the dark, the ones
who could have been you.

I reach out to stroke that lovely dip
they have, between haunch and hip,
the silk of their skin, that should
have been yours, and feel them recoil,
shivering, as if they have been touched
by knowing too much; by death.

When I send a token, my garland of jasmine
and a wisp of my hair, they pull back aghast
at the ring of white afloat on black
as if they can smell, braided in
to the scent of desire, the stench of loss,

as if they have felt the caress of a ghost.

Six pomegranate seeds

They burst on my tongue,
those seeds, when I ate them
one by one,

the taste of the world I remembered,
the colour of gardens
before I threw away the sun.

Underground

We have dug out this space
and buried ourselves here
before we die.

How can they call this battle,
when warriors are forced to lie
in burrows and scrabble in the dark

like tethered goats or mice?
Caged, we watch the moon
prowling through a mist of rain

and we are muttering
underground. In Punjabi
we are ourselves again.

Hira Singh slaps his thigh
or where his thigh once was,
and tells us the joke from Lyallpur.

Bhaga Singh is thinking of his wife
or her sarson da saag
at home in Ferozepur.

In his dreams,
Gurdit Singh is playing kabbadi
with the other boys in Gurdaspur.

We say the names
of our villages and towns
and know what we mean,

but not why we speak them here
in this frozen ground.
Only the rain

can hear what we are saying.
Sometimes it sounds like swearing.
Sometimes it sounds like praying.

The Letter

I am well.
I sleep on a charpoy
and think of you in the rain.

I go to the station
and wait for the train
that will bring you back.

When you bathed,
the sunlight trickled
down your face.

Stripped to the waist,
you poured water over
your long black hair.

If you were here
I would write my message
with fingers on your skin.

We have been too long apart.
How can I tell my heart
to the letter-writer?

Sixty seconds

Did you think I was gone?
You were wrong, I crossed back
out of water in that one minute
of black when a cloud passed the moon
and the moon looked away.
I bribed the gatekeeper

with six silver rings.

I am here in this room and have plotted
to keep you. I draw a ring
round your bed, surround you
with growing things, sheaves of wheat
and maize, sprouting seeds.
I break a coconut

and find, inside, another moon.

In your dreams I sleep with you,
breathing out when you breathe out,
breathing in when you breathe in,
stitching the night, stitching the air
stitching you in to spring.

Sticks

I make you again out of sticks and string,
bind you close and fix your face

with a stolen spider's web. Inside your head
I cage a small blue egg, and where your heart

should be, I tie a lump of lead.
This is how you live in my bed

and I in yours. She will never know,
except that one night you will call

my name and your hand will find itself
between my shadow legs. *Too late to stop.*

You will cheat her with me.
I will cheat death with art, with artifice,

my ghost voice whispering in your ear,
my spider words on your lips, *like this.*

Beak

I am trying to take this beak
out of my heart, this thing that troubles me
with its pecking, its demented singing.

In your living world, under the flame
of the forest, you stop
as if you have heard, and say, *Listen.*

Listen to that koel
calling.

Fix

It was loaded against me, the thing with the seeds.
They were there, just inside the skin, asking
to be eaten. Six pomegranate seeds,

six months in the light, six having sex
in the dark with a god I don't want.
I can't wait to get out to shops, the hot

bazaar, the baskets of peaches. I never know
if my voice reaches you, but I imagine you stopping
to look at your phone, checking missed calls,

caller unknown. Then you go on, out
of a station, crossing a road, my voice drowned
in the sound of car horns and the juice

exploding out of all those unfixed, living things.

Six rings

The phone rings six times.
You rarely answer the landline,
but tonight you pick up.
Static, crackling,
then my thin voice speaks
from a drowning world.

Others tune in, taking advantage
of the opening, crying over me,
wailing against the wall of white
sound, sending messages
for the people they still love,
the ones they left behind.

Tell my husband where to find
the thing I hid, in the cupboard,
top left shelf. Tell my daughter
to be kind. Tell my mother I didn't
mean it. Tell my lover I didn't
really mind.

You hear something, but far,
like a ghost with no throat,
like a shadow of words under water.

You never spoke to me, but did you see?
I wanted to tell you something, but something
tied my tongue. This is me, calling.

Rings

You sit at my table.
Through red wine, the sun sets
a ring on your finger.

You look out at the city
under its huge sky and ask
Do you get rainbows?

I do. I do.

A haunting of words

What are these words for?
What are they for, script

in every language, Spanish
Chinese Arabic, running

this way or that, from right to left,
from left to right, what right

do they have to be here
unless they force you to listen to

the bird in your heart and hear
the world as if it is new?

I am standing at the end
of the line, looking back at you

and past you to white.
Words are nothing

but gravestones unless they haunt
your day and night.

If you do not read the pulse
in my wrist I might

as well be gone.
Why put these marks on paper

at all if they do not twist
like a knife, prick like a thorn

buzz like a hive? What use,
unless they wire me alive?

Flight

Even if you have no name, I
will follow you down the steps
of the well, past the storied arches
to where the stones are green
with longing, and the water
wants us in.
                    You come
to the edge and look down,
the boys over your shoulder, just
watching. No wrong has been done.
I startle a bird, my feet
winged with fright,
                              the light
too long gone. My hand in the water
is all the drowned girls. You take it.
A flight of pale fingers, twined
so mine are yours, yours mine,
and we are an orchard
                              blossoming
under the waterskin.

Hell-raiser

Screeching out of the water,
screaming over the line,
I will be bawdy, tawdry, tough.
Laugh from the belly
when the holy men pass.
I am fearless,
striding back up the steps
into broad daylight.
Take off the white cloth
and fly like a kite
from the rooftops, and to hell
with the watchers, the talkers,
the gossips, the shame-peddlers.
I am out of their hands, blown
out of sight.

Haunted

Walls crack, a cloth flicks open
around a knot.
Glass splinters to moonlight.

Is that you? Don't drift away.
The trail of blood-red seeds
may lead to the words
we needed to say.
If this is haunting, let me be
haunted for ever. *Stay.*

Warning

The pomegranate gave me warning signs,
with its bitter rind, its thorny crown,
but I broke in through its forbidding

skin, tore away the thin membrane
to loot the seeds within. On my tongue
they exploded like nothing

I have ever known. On my lips the stain
remains. Even knowing what it means,
I would do it all again.

The trick

In a wasted time, it's only when I sleep
that all my senses come awake. In the wake
of you, let day not break. Let me keep
the scent, the weight, the bright of you, take
the countless hours and count them all night through
till that time comes when you come to the door
of dreams, carrying oranges that cast a glow
up into your face. Greedy for more
than the gift of seeing you, I lean in to taste
the colour, kiss it off your offered mouth.
For this, for this, I fall asleep in haste,
willing to fall for the trick that tells the truth
    that even your shade makes darkest absence bright,
    that shadows live wherever there is light.

Lapis Lazuli

If you thirst for blue beyond ultramarine,
here is the blue that stains the artist's hand,
lifted out of the most precious seam
in the generous heart of Badakshan

to place an azure light in the Pharaoh's eyes
after he is gone, lap at the Virgin's cloak,
seep into the masjid walls. A prize
to protect the wearer, allow the hope

that a simple ore could save the prey
and shield the savaged heart from harm;
that in a broken land it could find a way
to wrap the child in sacred blue, a charm

or talisman to still the approaching drone,
if you could only mine the prayer inside the stone.

The Elephant is walking on the River Thames

The whole city has come out to see the river
frozen over, solid enough to light a blazing fire
and spit-roast a whole ox, a suckling pig,
sparks in the air, fat hissing on silver,

mutton pies sizzling. Red-nosed boys
slide past St Paul's, horses pull sledges of coal
under the bridge, and then this:
an elephant steps carefully on to the ice.

The known world

cracks. Reality lumbers over the edge.
Hawkers freeze, pour ale into mid-air
as the creature sails by, more
graceful than any stilt-walker or skater.

Later they will recall it
like something suspended in time,
like first love at the last frost fair.
They will say, *That was the day. I was there.*

Hide

Scratches on crystal from scrabbling nails.
Scattered on ice are all the things
that fall from fingers and mouths
when the unknown walks in.

Dropped pie-crust, half-eaten pasty,
spilt gin, broken bottle, cracked cup,
caught up in the drama of this coming.
Its body wrinkles in the folds

like someone old or very new, like a person
they may know. They lift their hands
but do not touch, as if to pat the space
around its flanks and rump.

Between hovering palms and elephant hide,
a blessing freezes on rapt air.

First sight, through falling snow

The elephant looks
at the cathedral. It looks
back. Their hearts tangle.

Fair

That was the winter
   the Thames froze over
      for the very last time.

The last time she saw him she said
   (and she meant it) she would
      love him till hell froze over.

Over time, the earth grew warmer,
   they widened the arches.
      These reasons came later.

Later she couldn't remember
   the reasons. It felt true enough
      at that moment.

The moment the tides ran faster,
   too fast for ice, the frost and the fairs
      melted back into water.

Back then, they could not have known
   that whatever it was
      it would never happen again.

Night vision

The camera shows you, in green,
what it was to be there. Faces
float up out of a noisy frame,
pale flowers blossom on twisted stalks,
not themselves but a memory of themselves
with red and blue drained away,
like things left in the water too long.

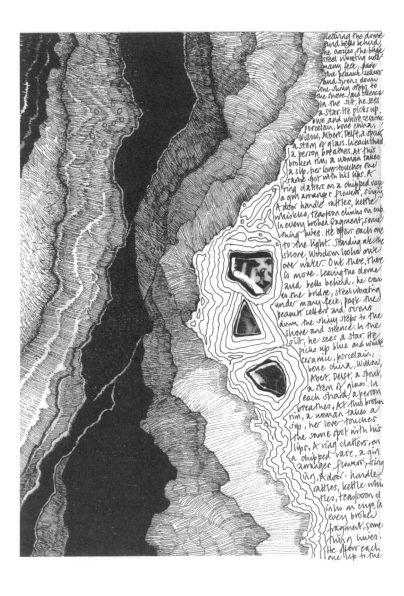

Mr Wisdom Looks for China by the Thames

Leaving the dome and bells behind,
he crosses the bridge, steel ringing

under his feet, past
the peanut sellers and sirens

down the slimy steps to the shore
and silence. In the silt, he sees a star.

He picks up blue and white
porcelain, slipware, bone,

willow, majolica, delft –
and others, impossible to classify,

sliding off china, parts of animals
that could belong to an emperor,

lion's mane, elephant's eye,
serpent's tail,

some that, from a distance,
resemble flies

drawn with a fine camel's-hair brush
on a spout, a lid, a stem of glass.

Off the edge, a person breathes.
At this rim, a woman takes a sip,

her lover touches the same spot
with his lips. A girl

arranges flowers in a vase
that is about to break.

A door-handle rattles,
teaspoon clinks on cup,

in chip and sliver, something lives.
He offers each one to the light.

Standing at the shore, Wisdom looks out
over water. Out there, there is more.

Larks

Mr Wisdom is meticulous, gloved
against disease, sharpies,

burger wraps, tin cans. He scrapes
no more than an inch in.

Out of another time,
smaller fingers are digging down,

rummaging deep for rusty nails, brass
buttons, coal, anything that will buy a pie.

By the dangerous river, the venomous mud,
they ferret, turn a fragment over,

discard it, wipe snot. Mr Wisdom's hand
is real, for now at least, but theirs are not.

In spite of this, they catch at his ankles,
trip him up. On a jagged edge, he tears a sleeve,

blood drips down an arm. Mr Wisdom
knows it is only larks. No harm done.

When he finds a copper coin, he leaves it there
for a hand that wants it more.

Heavenly Emporium

He takes the pieces of china home
and places them together, not

to recreate the thing
they were, but to make

a shape wiser than a cup or plate,
the broken edges uncontained

and patient enough to lie in wait
for the tide to turn, for the full moon.

If you are looking for Wisdom

Go down to the foreshore
any afternoon in fair weather

or foul, when the tide is out,
through the gurgle of water

on pebbles and cobbles,
and you will find him there,

where the slow boats
come and go,

still looking for china.

m) Those that have just broken the vase

The vase too perfect,
its roses so well-disposed.
My hands let it go.

Then the drone, the hush.
The bomb came, looking
for something to kill.
The me it chose as prey
was you as if play
made them to be lives
with a fist of stone the weight
of a war come down on you

Fallen, you
are statue-still.
This has not happened
to a lump of metal,
but to a body
that looks like
a child's.

It dents the heart.

Cherub, St Paul's

You were made to float in equal light,
at ease, your hands behind your head.
Swung high on praise in the sight of God,
you witnessed every prayer said, telling
your time by matins and by evensong, wild
bells ringing. You seemed, even cast in bronze
to have no weight, or only the weight of a child,
flesh rounded over bird-light bones.

Then the drone, the hush. The bomb
came looking for something to kill.
It never saw the virgin, and glanced away
from the form of Christ, already crucified.
The one it chose as prey was you, at play,
wide open to its anger. With a fist of stone
the weight of a war came down on you.
Your ribs caved in where you took the blow.

Fallen, you are statue still.
This has not happened to a lump of metal,
but to a body that looks like a child's.

It dents the heart.

What are we to make of you?
A guardian, a bruised miracle, thrown
into the nave or on to today's front page,

the child who saved us,
the child we could have saved,
if we had been looking, if
we had been paying attention? In the aftermath,

the hesitant dust falls back to blanket you,
rubble tries to cradle you. Just
as we turn away, light seeks out your mouth
and wipes it with stained fingers. It takes the shine,

the refractions from your crumpled wound
and carries them up the columns
to rooftops that are waiting to be mended,
cratered streets and alleyways to be undented.
To the builders, the hammerers,
the crane operators and carpenters,
the engineers and makers,
it opens its fingers and offers

all it has to offer, the sigh
it took from you,
the lightness,
the stain of blue.

Checkout

Before you wake you know the window has shifted
across the room from the left of the bed to the right.
As your eyes open you know the world has been lifted
and tilted into an unaccustomed light.

You turn and stretch and take a breath. The sheet
breathes back, a new-made scent. Sent here, laid
down in a white elsewhere, you get up to meet
the mirror that has been hung too high, the unmade

person craning into it, different
today from the ones who came this way before,
risen out of the same bed, indifferent
strangers. Together, you prepare to open the door,

but cast a look back into the uncomplicated space
behind you, the transitory moment of grace.

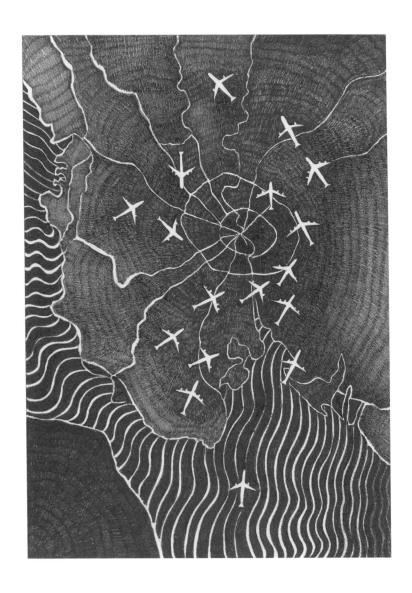

Flight Radar

From the top of the Shard the view unfolds
down the Thames to the sea, the city laid
by a trick of sight vertically in front of me.
At London Bridge Station, trains slide in

and out in a long slow dance. It is not
by chance that I am here, not looking down
but up to where you are on Flight 199,
coming in to land. I have learned to track you

on my mobile phone. However far you go,
I have the app that uses the radar to trace
your path. There you are now, circling down
around this spire where I stand, my face reflected

over your pulse in the glass. You cannot see.
You have no radar for me, no app to make you
look back or down to where I am lifting my hand.
Darling, I will track your flight till it is a dot

that turns and banks and falls out of sight, looking
into the space where you were. Fingers frozen
on the tiny keys, I will stay where I am
in the dying light, the screen still live in my palm.

Unexploded

Like a giant boar, pig-ugly, it tore
out of the sky with its load

of death. Clumsy, it missed the mark
and snouted down into the road

snuffling the hem of the cathedral, too close,
too close. Unexploded, but eager to explode.

The saints held their breath, bells
bit their tongues, singing died.

Streets were emptied,
trams hushed, children sent away to hide.

The men dug their way to it,
pushing down to the monstrous thing inside,

wet cloth wound around their faces
against the murderous fumes, gases

let loose out of the city's punctured intestines.
Hours ticked by. Three days ticked by.

Three men down, twenty-seven feet in,
they worked around its lethal flanks.

Sapper Wyllie and the squad
were gentle, gentler than midwives

when they brought it out, slick and slippery
as any newborn, the one-ton bomb.

Lieutenant Davies drove the beast,
its heart still ticking, across London,

past gaping houses, to the east.
There, in Hackney Marshes, at last

the creature's body was allowed to burst.
It blew a mirror image in the earth

of the thing it could not destroy,
a crater that might have been

the size of a cathedral, a crater
that could have taken the shape of a dome,

the scar of its intention overcome,
in time, with ragwort, cow parsley, burdock,

blurred by chaffinch and sparrowhawk,
an explosion of wings come home.

Exploded

A prayer is said,
a story told. Under the dome
the Word explodes.

Channel of vision

Photograph SPCAA/P/1/4/24

The apostles have climbed up on the roof to look
at the world in black and white, the strut

of warehouses by the river, bridges, barges,
plundered cargo at the wharves.

Sunset burns the skyline down to size.
By sunrise it is back on its feet again

with billboards for Bovril,
Breakfasts Dinners Teas at Turner's,

the logos of banks climbing up Ludgate Hill.
The city draws its ambition on unused air,

and plots its future until
it stands there, concrete.

Clouds bunch together and mutter
darkly, threaten a riot

against barefaced glass,
the rise and rise that eats the sky.

Matthew, Mark, Luke, John, Paul
have seen it all: fortunes rise and fortunes fall.

Everything that lives will change.
Nothing is fixed except for the photograph

numbered and dated by the careful archivist.
Mist rubs out the horizon. It has no memory

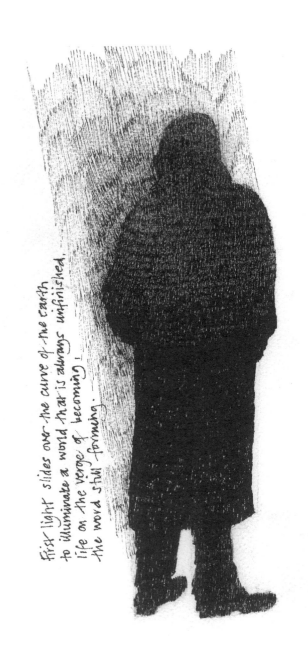

First light slides over the curve of the earth
to illuminate a world that is always unfinished.
Life on the verge of becoming,
the word still forming.

of itself, or only the memory of an optimist.
Highbury and Islington swoop down to Smooth Fields,

scattering meadow flowers. Farringdon Street
turns itself back into the River Fleet.

The fragments are arranged
and rearranged

but for the watchers on the roof
there is no impediment,

no then or there or here.
The sightline is clear.

First light slides over the curve of the earth
to illuminate a world that is always unfinished,

life on the verge of becoming,
the word still forming.

Brutal

It sails up out of the City, a ship
whose prow is angled to the jagged sky,
eager to strike out on its own, defy
the ordinary and travel to the lip

of what is possible. The tower has found a way
out of rubble, the aftershock, the grief
of repeated history and lost belief,
to lift up the passer's face and say

this is the place marked out for peace
in the city's troubled heart, so it may beat
again without brutality. Released

to blue, untethered from the street
by engineers and architects, this is a piece
of hope they dared to take and make concrete.

The Elephants are on the Piccadilly Line

The elephants are travelling underground,
tilting gently as the train careens.
No one sees them, all the heads bent down
to worship information on small screens.

Perhaps the elephants wonder at how still
the people sit or how the light shines blue through
human eyelashes, or admire their digital skill
on keyboards, too neat for elephant toes, too

small for trunks. Google cannot contain
the wisdom of elephants. The whole of the internet
cannot fathom one spark of the elephant brain.
So they come swaying through Russell Square, to set

foot here, tail to trunk, trunk to tail,
like aliens, like gods who may not fail.

Be aware
the fabricks
will decay.
Take away
the stone,
lift from the head
the weight. Born
to light the hidden
face. Find
inside the
resonating space,
the way to hear
the living poem.

90

The Fabrick

Look up at the vast span of the drum,
the lantern's height, the dome.
See how the architect lifted the weight
of all this magnificence away

from foundations laid on uneasy clay,
the shifting earth, the splitting skin,
the frailty of rubble at the core.
Be aware the fabrick will decay.

Take ye away the stone.

Lift from the heart the weight.
Bring to light the hidden face.
Find, inside the resonating space,
the way to live, the living poem.

Ringing the changes

Twelve bells were donated to St Paul's,
many by the Livery Companies of London

The market has lost its sound track,
no vans from Scotland or Wales unloading
their stock, hooks swinging, doors slamming,
shutters banged back. All the usual effing

and blinding has stopped for the day. A walk away,
twelve bells have found tongues. The clapper strikes
for the Company of Drapers, treble as hangers
on rails, flicking a tail to the Fishmongers
in a shiver of scales. The Grocers sing out
on a note you could eat, seasoned by Salters.
Clothworkers shuttle it on to the Taylors
over six days of toil, singing looms, oinking pigs,
lowing cattle. The ring goes full circle from treble
to tenor, tenor to treble, all the world's trouble
turned around on a peal of pure sound.

The tower is alive with it, the air vibrates
with the thrust and the weight
of bells being swung, the changes rung
from the top of St Paul's.

The city's business becomes
a calling of bells.

The sound of your name

The city is silenced, holding its breath
as if it is waiting for something to shift,
for summer to become summer
in a month battered by winds, set adrift,

and the sky inconsolable, weeping.

Our hearts' climate has changed
to winter. We are bereft.
But grief makes believers even of those
who would not believe. We lift

up our heads to seek the reprieve,

the green song in the trees. We picture you
strong, walking ahead of us into the sun,
turning to look at us, leading the way
as you always did. Grief gives this gift,

the belief that you do not stop

but walk on in our love and grow on
in the children. They will play you back to us,
that voice, that laugh. You will be there
on the sound track when we celebrate,

you will be present in our conversation.

Even those of us who do not believe
will believe, when the trees take a breath
that sounds like your name
whispered into our hearts' great microphone.

The season will change and we will give thanks

that we knew you.
We will know you in any season,
winter or summer, summer or winter,
and we will have reason

to believe that you do not stop.

Bloom

You are nothing more than yourself,
not a message sent to change the world,
not here to save mankind or even me. You are,

like a snail or mollusc, only there;
like a leaf among thousands on a tree,
like the sea or the smallest of its creatures,

just there. And yet, and yet I watch your face
and see a star waking in your eyes
like sap-rise to a leaf, tide-rush to the moon.

I try to live the life inside your head, think
what you are thinking, feel what makes
your heart beat fast, small body, small weight

in my arms. More than my self, I want to know
you. This is the gift you give. Cradling you close
I feel the world and all its waking life.

Holding you, I hold the world,
wishing it for ever safe.

Close to the sun

(for a child, not yet three)

When a starling rises from a line, stirring
the flock to new-found words, when a raucous crow
flings itself off the ground, your questioning
begins. *Where did it come from, where did it go,*

will it reach the sun, will it burn, will it touch the moon
or be lost in starholes? Why do I have skin
and not feathers, when will I grow wings? How soon?
You pursue anything that flies, a robin,

magpie, butterfly, helicopter, plane.
Some upward surge of the blood makes you believe
the sky is yours. Beak at the window-pane,
on one leg, you flap your arms to heave

away from ground. You can hardly breathe.
I need. I need to fly! I hold you
while I can before you learn to leave.

Wolf, Words

In another room, the children are pigs.
You can hear them truffling behind sofas,
bumping chairs, snuffling round table-legs.

From the dregs of a story, the wolf
inks in, pulled to the sound of breathing,
drawn to the warm, the living,

rasping, *Let me in. Let me in.*
In their literal world, the children believe
the wolf is a wolf not a wolf made of words.

They make themselves small behind closed doors
in a house made of straw and a house made of sticks
and a house made of bricks, in a time

made of tricks. But the breath of the wolf
is the breath of the world. It blows a flurry
of straw, a volley of twigs, a fall

of rubble down on the pigs
who come squealing, squalling out of the storm
to a house made of words. This.

Scratching at walls, something is out there,
ever and after, something that howls.
What outcast word, what unhoused soul?

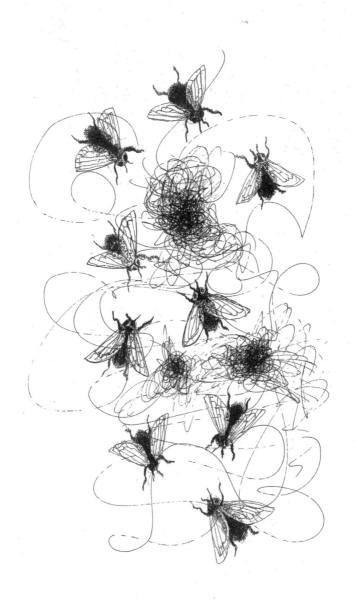

What will you tell the children?

Step into the light. The microphone is ready
to deliver your words to the dark.

They have arrived to hear you. They could
be out in the park, their faces turned up

to the sun. Instead they are in here,
not loud but rustling, squirming

and breathing, heaving, live.
How much have they lived?

Enough to know that behind them
the colour of words has changed?

What will you tell them: that we used up our heroes
and the ones left over are those who lied

best, that our dreams were alive
but we took them for granted and then they died

and came back in bin-bags,
that someone lit a spark and we snuffed it out?

What can you tell the children?
They are out there, waiting in the dark.

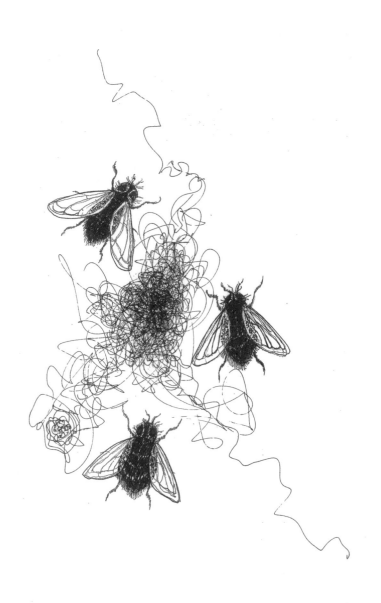

Out of line

Happy arrives with the moon on its shoulder. Glamorous.
You can tell it has crossed the line by the way it moves,
eyes glittering like wet roads in headlights, dangerous
and out of control, attention all over the place. It loves

the language and talks to strangers, asks your name,
looks in your face and offers its hand, no sign of a knife
or a gun, no respect for the rules, not a trace of shame.
Before you can stop it, Happy slaps your back and kisses your wife

on the cheek. This is no place for Happy. It leads to touching.
it could spread an infection, cause a contagion of glances
with that dirty laugh, wine on the breath, it encourages smiling
and unrestricted movement of hands and feet. Dances.

Happy is just asking to be buried up to its neck in sand,
a face like that, asking to be stoned

to death. Is Happy known to you? Tell Happy this
for its own good, to hide its ankles, cover its wrists.

Gurh and ghee

Would he have had a son
who looked like him?

No one can stop these things happening.
A clay cup will smash on the station platform,

a bucket will break in the well,
a bullet will find a body, and explode,

but is there anyone here to say
that he was some mother's son,

who remembers that I fed him
gurh and ghee? Is there anyone?

The Jump

At last he comes out of his room
and his skin is webbed, his face masked

in red, but I can see where he has sewn
the pieces of polyester together,

and where he has zipped himself in.
When I squeeze this super-hero's arm

he is still my boy inside,
nothing but bone.

Come for food, I say, *khaman-dhoklas are hot,*
aunties and uncles are waiting.

But he says, *If somebody told you it was easy*
to grow another skin, they lied.

So we are in the sitting-room,
hunger rumbling, the smell of food

calling from the kitchen, watching him
jump off the sofa. He is whispering,

Go web! Up, up and away, web!
Shazam!

Then, knees bent to his chest,
he sails over Bolton,

Leicester, Brent, New York.
The carpet becomes a map of the world

and in front of my eyes he is owning
this other skin, crossing a line.

He is strange and beautiful,
and no longer mine.

Send this

Do not send me a postcard
of the city that once lived here,
its water-courses and its domes.
No photograph can show that this
was once home, and that home
is long gone.

Do not send me a miniature
drawn with a camel's-hair brush
to hang on my wall, or tell me
you were in the Anarkali Bazaar,
or say the gulmohar trees were aflame
and koels sang there.

Everything changes. Remind me
of this when the light falls aslant
on things not quite made, girders laid
over half-drawn plans, haggled over
and paid, the truth retold and sold
in new-built malls.

With the wrong key, I come
to this place and try to unlock it.
Air-conditioners rattle and spit
at the back of suburban villas.
Someone here has built a room,
left space for a window,

opened a door, a desire.
Do not mock it. In an almost-done
world, send me this, knowing
nothing is ever fixed. I will carry
the unfinished walls of my city
with me, in my pocket.

This line, that thread

Draw a line from finger to heart.
Draw the water from well to mouth.
Place a mark where the words were said,
map the distance from north to south.

Take it apart and start again.

Look out of the window at your neighbour.
Look in the mirror at your own face.
Breathe on the glass to blur the border,
watch it become an unowned space.

Wipe it away and begin again.

Hold the end of a single thread,
loop it to others, weave it to lace.
Spread it out to see if the holes
are an imperfection or a kind of grace

with their open heart, their otherness.

The garden gnomes are on their mobile phones

Headphones on, the gnomes
will never know the sound

of the common yarrow
trying to grow.

The plumbago can hardly hear itself
think over passing buses, sirens, drills,

washing machines, tumble dryers,
beeping tills.

The gnomes are online
or out at the shops, buying

portable speakers, voice recognition
software, high-top sneakers,

not caring if the lobelia is trying
to breathe over the harsh kiss

of pesticide and sewage
spewed out from factories.

The gnomes are busy
watching *Game of Thrones*,

jamming buttons on controllers,
checking their likes on mobile phones.

For the basil, time moves in slow-motion
and the gnomes are a passing blur.

The money plant and marigold
are in conversation. They remember

a time when there was water nearby
and they could sense it,

a time before cars and their fumes,
before gnomes.

The world is in the tiny hands
of those with cash hidden

under the flower-beds, or stashed
in socks.

The garden gnomes are devious.
They are singing

lullabies
to the unsuspecting phlox.

Drain

What comes out of this place
is rust-coloured water, mountains of scraps
tossed away, the after-taste of excess
on the tongue, the long squirm
of it in the heart, the lurch of too much.

All this should lurk and hide, but
it is out there on show like a wedding party
with dancers, brass bands, flaunting
itself to the world. *This is how much
I can afford*, it says, *to throw away.*

Out with drums pounding,
tassels shaking, all the red and gold
in the world weighing down the bride
till she is on her knees, saying
Please, but not finishing, exhausted

by the whole thing, by being sold
out. Struggling out of cracks
are the hands that are too small, not
reaching up for help, not reaching,
because what is there but air,

and even that used up, drained?

Double

You have a double life. You run away to live
with a dour man in Casablanca, and huddle
with a surly angel on the rooftops of Berlin.

There is another you, stalking
a blue raincoat through the bars of New York,
so close you can smell the gabardine.

You follow footsteps down an alley
as streetlights come on, to a fairground
guttering in the rain. The other life

plays a sound track of its own,
a single voice, a saxophone. It happens
in the pages of a book

where huge birds wheel, ships set sail
over jewelled ports. There is a woman
who keeps a murdering king awake all night.

She tells a story that cannot end,
in a language you have never learned,
but in the double life, you understand.

3 a.m., the radio on

The sound is tossing, turning,
winding the sheet, a wave
to drown in. No solid ground
but the swell of gone; the heave and hope
of the folded note, a paper boat.

One frame of black, the moon put out,
the crumpled cargo delivered
to the shore. The surge retreats,
turns back to what it was before,
a winding sheet.

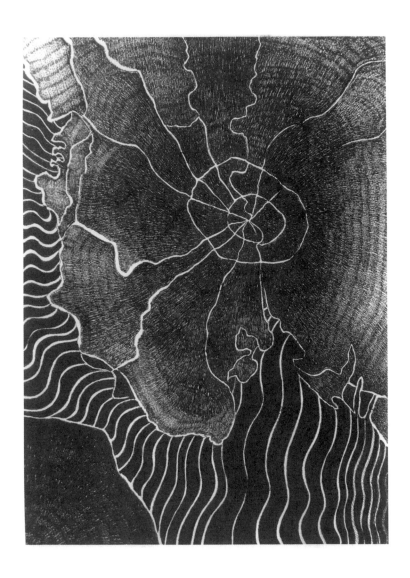

Estuary

You plan to leave as soon as you arrive.
Five years later you look around and find

you are still here. You might think
this is the kind of place where nothing happens

but for a place where nothing happens
everything is going on. Not Paris

or New York or Rome, but a town
that leaves you well alone.

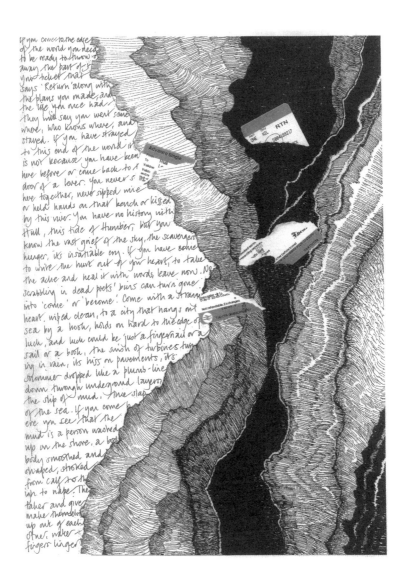

If you come to the edge
of the world you need
to be ready to throw
away the part of
your ticket that
says 'Return' along with
the plans you made, and
the life you once had.
They will say you went some
where, who knows where, and
stayed. If you have strayed
to this end of the world it
is not because you have been
here before or come back to the
door of a lover you never s
here together, never sipped wine
or held hands on that bench or kissed
by this river. You have no history with
Hull, this tide of Humber, but you
know the vast grief of the sky, the scavengers
hunger, its insatiable em. If you have come
to write the hurt out of your heart, to take
the ache and heal it with words, leave now. No
scrabbling in dead poets' bins can turn 'gone'
into 'come' or 'become'. Come with a strain
heart, wiped clean, to a city that hangs out
sea by a hook, holds on hard to the edge of
luck, and luck could be just a fingernail or a
sail or a book, the swish of turbines turn
ing in rain, its hiss on pavements, its
shimmer dropped like a plumb-line
down through underground layers,
the slip of mud, the slap
of the sea. If you come
ere you see that the
mud is a person washed
up on the shore, a be
body smoothed and
swaded, stroked
from calf to th
igh to nape. The
taker and give
make themselve
up out of each
other, water
fingers linger

This Tide of Humber

If you come to the edge of the world
you need to be ready to throw away

the part of your ticket that says *Return*
along with the plans you made, and the life

you once had. They will say you went
somewhere, who knows where, and stayed.

If you have strayed to this end of the world
it is not because you have been here before

or come back to the door of a lover.
You never sat here together, never

sipped wine or held hands on that bench
or kissed by this river.

You have no history with Hull,
this tide of Humber,

but you know the vast grief
of the sky, the scavenger's hunger,

its insatiable cry.
If you have come to write the hurt

out of your heart, to take the ache
and heal it with words, leave now.

No scrabbling in dead poets' bins
can turn *gone* into *come* or *become*.

Come with a stranger's heart, wiped clean,
to a city that hangs on the sea by a hook,

holds on hard to the edge of luck,
and luck could be

just a fingernail
or a sail or a book,

the swish of turbines turning in rain,
its hiss on pavements, its shimmer

dropped like a plumb-line, down
through underground layers,

the slip of mud,
the slap of the sea.

If you come here you see
that the mud is a person washed up

on the shore, a body smoothed and shaped,
stroked from calf to thigh to nape.

The taker and giver
make themselves up out of each other,

water-fingers linger in the deepest folds,
limbs open and close back into the river,

an arm or a leg or a hip
heave out from under the sheet.

The lifted mud is only a hint
of the lost land beneath,

between the shorelines
that yearn for each other.

Water and mud,
mud and water, intricate lovers.

You stand here and hope
that a hand will lift out

of a wave, wave to you
from that weather-drowned land.

Even your stranger's feet remember
pacing the ground under the water,

the tracks of women and men, crossing,
criss-crossing after ice and drought,

through storm and calm, hunting
the sun and rain, scents on the wind.

You were never looking for ghosts
but they find you here.

Voices sing through the tide.
The rustling, the breathing, the music

of travellers takes you out where the land
would have been, walked over, washed away,

rolled in. And there, the ghost hulls
of the trawlers nudge out of the dark

with the trawlermen who never came back,
hauling their own white wake

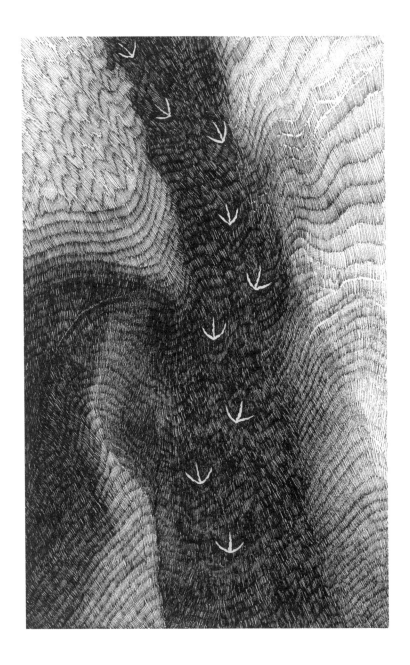

and their catch, the fish crying silver
in nets made of air.

If you come to the end of the world
it stings like the edge of a blade,

the verge of a cut, but the cut is a freedom,
a severed rope. Freed men and women

rise up and walk out of the water
and you go with them

past the docks, past terraces and tanneries
with a crowd that grows in every lane,

that dares to look down on a king,
swings up Hessle Road, along

the Boulevard, the Avenue
and Terry Street, past the Minster

and fish market to the Deep,
through a city bombed and bruised,

razed flat, raised up again.
It spreads a grey wing, leads you

to the smallest window you have ever seen,
and through it, shows you all the world,

takes your food, makes it a feast,
holds your stranger's body, folds it

in arms of mud,
and the gulls walk over your heart,

over and over, return, repeat,
on hieroglyph feet, their tracks

a braille of messages
delivered from half-built edges.

The water seeps over the drowned land
to the lip of the city.

It holds its breath.
The women stop

their washing, their stirring, their kneading
and pounding to listen.

Between the widowed face of the sky
and the ringed eye of a gull

everything changes scale.
A blade of grass is a turbine wing

that lifts to the light as a fish
gleams under the blade of an oar

like a shoulder blade
kissed by the moon,

and the land wears the water like a shining veil,
and the water bears the moon like a sacred jewel,

and the heart is a fish
and luck is the hook

that flicks it up between water and land,
between Humber and Hull

and holds it there
at the edge of the world.

ACKNOWLEDGEMENTS

Some of these poems first appeared in: *Railway Nation: A Journey in Verse* (BBC 2, 2016); *Winter Solstice Poems* (BBC Radio 4, 2017), *On Shakespeare's Sonnets: A Poets' Celebration*, ed. Hannah Crawforth and Elizabeth Scott-Baumann (Bloomsbury Arden Shakespeare 2016); *Ploughshares: transatlantic poetry issue*, ed. Neil Astley (2015); *Through the Door* (Poet in the City and Archives for London, 2015); *The Wenlock Poetry Festival Anthology*; *Hwaet! 20 Years of Ledbury Poetry Festival*, ed. Mark Fisher (Bloodaxe Books, 2016); *Scotia Extremis Whaur Extremes Meet* (2016); *Six Poems North and South* (Manchester Literature Festival, 2017), 'Poetry Rocks', *The Economist 1843* (2014).

With thanks to Canon Mark Oakley, Sarah Radford, Jo Wisdom, Simon Carter, Teresa Heady and Donna McDowell of St Paul's Cathedral, and especially to Mr Wisdom for allowing me to use his name as well as the blue and white china; Kirsty Young for pointing the way back to unfinished business in Glasgow; Andy Jackson and Brian Johnstone of *Scotia Extremis*; James House, Alistair Pegg and Joe Fowler of Blast! Films for their unfailing energy and many round-trips London-Glasgow-London; Isobel Colchester of Poet in the City; the ever-inventive Nima Poovaya-Smith, Umi Mistry, David Lascelles of Alchemy Leeds, with Christella Litras, Rob Green, Richard Littlewood, Jack Lockhart; Leeds Old Library and the staff and students of Leeds School of Art; Kamini Banga for leading me to the stepped well, Agrasen ki Baoli, in Delhi; Sue Roberts and BBC *Contains Strong Language*, Martin Green and all those involved with Hull City of Culture, Jackie Goodman, the JoinedUp Dance Company and Joe Roper; Robert Seatter, John

Broadbent, Sonia McKay, Lucia Yandoli for the songs; David Benfold, Carol Stevens and especially Andrea Kidd for the image that led to 'Flight Radar'; the family of Hannah Andrassey, Steve Escritt, Polly and Lexie; Cathy Bolton, Manchester Literature Festival and Manchester Art Gallery; Anna Dreda and the Wenlock Poetry Festival; Nicholas Crane for his wisdom; Rachel Dwyer and SOAS; Neil Astley and everyone at Bloodaxe for support that always goes far beyond the everyday; Vicky Edwards, Stella Fearnley and Huw Evans of Poetry Live!, Gillian Clarke, Jackie Kay, Daljit Nagra, Simon Armitage, John Agard, Grace Nichols, Owen Sheers and Maura Dooley for the continuing inspiration on the road; Sean McGrath, Rita McGrath and Helen Taylor; all my families around the world: the Mobariks in Scotland; Minal and Rani Dharker, and the Dilkhush family in India; Jean Powell and three generations of Powells in Wales; Gareth Powell and Shinae Won in South Korea; Shahnaz and Jim Lambert, Iwan Powell, Becky Gilbey, Robert and Ava Taylor, Daniel, Lucia, Luca and Sofia Powell and the extended Powell-Dharker-Taylor-Yandoli family; and with very special thanks to Carol Ann Duffy and Ayesha Dharker for more reasons than I can count.

Imtiaz Dharker grew up a Muslim Calvinist in a Lahori household in Glasgow, was adopted by India and married into Wales. She is an accomplished artist and documentary film-maker, and has published six collections with Bloodaxe in Britain, all including her own drawings: *Postcards from god* [including *Purdah*] (1997), *I speak for the devil* (2001), *The terrorist at my table* (2006) *Leaving Fingerprints* (2009), *Over the Moon* (2014) and *Luck is the Hook* (2018). She was awarded the Queen's Gold Medal for Poetry 2014.